Up the Garden Path

Are you a Snail?

KINGFISHER
Kingfisher Publications Plc
New Penderel House
283–288 High Holborn
London WC1V 7HZ

First published by Kingfisher Publications Plc 2000

2 4 6 8 10 9 7 5 3 1

1TR/1199/TWP/DIG(DIG)/150NYMA

A CIP catalogue record for this book is available from
the British Library.

ISBN 0 7534 041 4

Editor: Katie Puckett
Series Designer: Jane Tassie

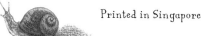

Printed in Singapore

Up the Garden Path

Are You a Snail?

Judy Allen and Tudor Humphries

KING*f*ISHER

Are you a snail?

If you are, your life began in
an egg like one of these.

When you hatch, you look like this.
This is your mother.

You are much smaller
than your mother.

You are very, very small,

but you will grOW.

You have two horns and two
eyes on stalks.

You can pull your eyes right down
inside the stalks and into your
head if you need to.

You are slimy. You are VERY slimy.

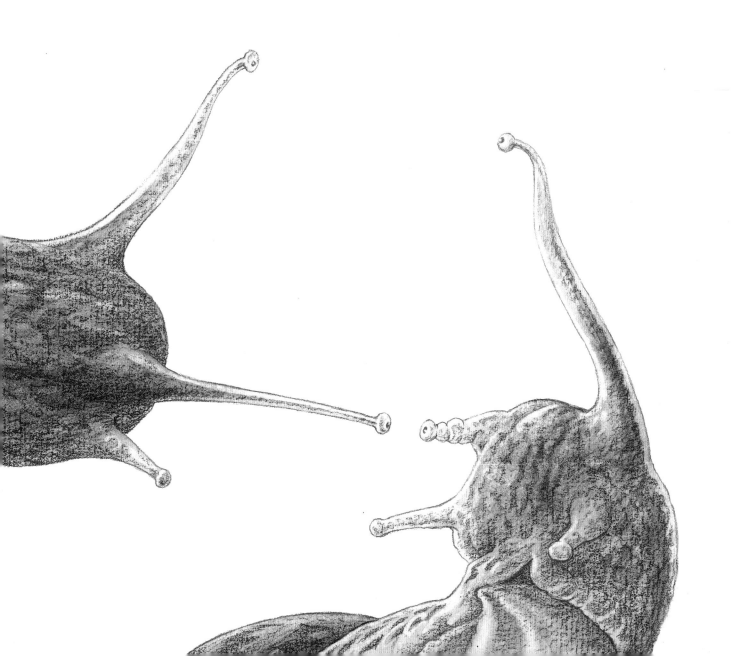

You have a shell
with a beautiful
pattern on it.

You have no
legs and only
one foot, but it
is a strong foot.

The slime on your strong
foot helps you to
slide along.

Wherever you go,
you leave a silvery slimy trail.

You like damp places.

You like to be out
when it has rained.

You have a big, rough tongue right inside your mouth. Use it to rip pieces off leaves and eat them.

Look out for thrushes.

Thrushes are dangerous.

They like to eat snails.

They know how to break the shells off,
and they don't mind the slime.

Hide in the daytime. Go out at night
when the thrushes are asleep.

Look out for foxes.

Foxes are dangerous.

Hungry foxes eat snails and they don't mind the slime either.

Foxes go out at night, but you can't hide at night because you need to eat sometime. Just be careful.

Do not walk where humans walk.
You could get squashed. You move
too slowly to get out of the way.

Humans don't like you because you
eat their plants. They may put poison
or sharp grit in the garden.

It hurts to walk on grit.
Also, grit sticks to your slime.

And poison? Poison is poisonous!

You may meet someone who looks like this.

It is not a snail whose shell has fallen off. This is a slug.

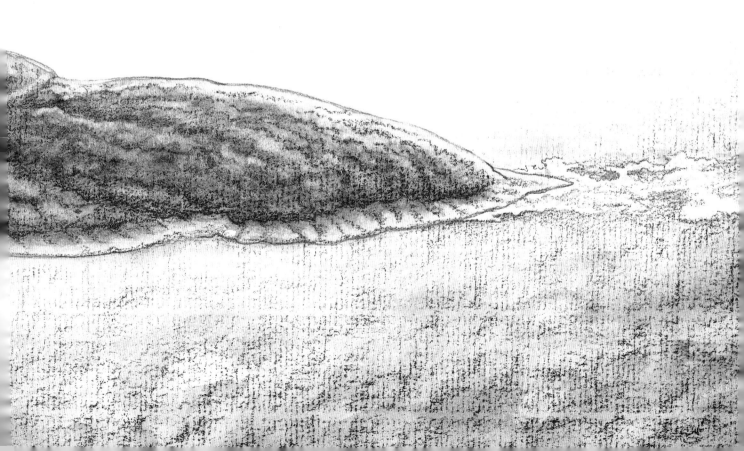

The winter cold makes
you sleepy. Find a hiding place.

Your slime hardens into
a door in your shell.

The spring warmth
wakes you. Dribble on the
inside of your shell door. It melts away.

Slime off and find food.

However, if you look a bit

or this

like this   or this

or this

you are

not a snail.

You are...

...a human child.

You have no shell on your back.
You have no horns and your
eyes are not on stalks.

Never mind, you can do a great many
things a snail can't do.

Also, you are not afraid
of thrushes or foxes.

Most humans like you.

Best of all, you are not
in the least bit
slimy.

Did You Know...

...The trail of a snail is broken up but the trail of a slug is one long line of slime.

...There are more than 60,000 different kinds of snail.

...This is a garden snail but there are other kinds who live in deserts or swamps, in ponds or rivers, or in the sea.

...The Giant
African snail
can grow very large.
The biggest one ever found was 40cm
long and weighed 900 grams.

...Snails belong to a family of creatures
called 'gastropods' which
means stomach-foot.
So you could say a snail is a
stomach on a
foot.

31